INTRODUCTION

Welcome to the No-Spend & Savings Journal, the ideal tool for taking charge of your money and making saving fun! In order to help you keep aware of your spending patterns, this journal includes a monthly no-spend tracker where you can record your budget, motivations, temptations, exceptions and rewards.
It also comes with weekly and monthly savings trackers, making it simple for you to keep track of how far you've come in reaching your saving goals. There's also a fun savings game included to keep you engaged and inspired as you accumulate money.

To support you on your path to financial wellness, our savings journal also includes useful savings tips. The undated pages allow you to start using it whenever you want and keep track of your progress for up to three years. This savings journal will help you reach your financial goals by improving your awareness of your spending patterns, setting attainable savings goals, and tracking your progress.

Your opinion matters to us, and we'd love to hear it! By sharing your experience, you can help us to improve our products. We would greatly appreciate it if you would take 2 minutes to leave us a review on Amazon.

10 TIPS TO DO A NO-SPEND MONTH

1. Create and keep to a budget for your no-spend month. This will assist you in setting spending priorities and preventing wasteful spending.

2. Prepare your meals in advance and steer clear of takeaway or eating out. You'll be able to reduce your food expenses as a result.

3. Make use of what you already have rather than purchasing new goods. This includes personal items, furniture, and entertainment.

4. Reduce travel costs: Reduce travel costs by carpooling, using public transit, or biking or walking whenever practical.

5. Cancel unused memberships: Do not keep any memberships or subscriptions that you are not utilizing. This will enable you to reduce your monthly expenses.

6. Utilize free entertainment options: Consider going to museums, parks, or free local activities as examples of free entertainment.

7. Don't go shopping: Don't go shopping for things that aren't necessary, such as accessories, gadgets, and clothing. Limit yourself to the necessities for daily life.

8. Try borrowing or exchanging products with friends or family members rather than purchasing new ones. This will enable you to cut back on waste and save money.

9. Resist the urge to shop online by unsubscribing from marketing emails, blocking shopping websites, and avoiding online advertisements.

10. Discover inventive methods to make money: During your no-spend month, think of inventive ways to make money, such as by selling goods you no longer need, accepting freelancing work, or conducting paid surveys.

No-Spend
TRACKER

DAILY NO-SPEND TRACKER

1	2	3	4	5
6	**7**	**8**	**9**	**10**
11	**12**	**13**	**14**	**15**
16	**17**	**18**	**19**	**20**
21	**22**	**23**	**24**	**25**
26	**27**	**28**	**29**	**30**
31	**TOTAL**			

BUDGET

MOTIVATIONS

TEMPTATIONS

EXCEPTIONS

REWARDS

DAILY NO-SPEND TRACKER

1	2	3	4	5
6	7	8	9	10
11	12	13	14	15
16	17	18	19	20
21	22	23	24	25
26	27	28	29	30
31	TOTAL			

BUDGET

MOTIVATIONS

TEMPTATIONS

EXCEPTIONS

REWARDS

DAILY NO-SPEND TRACKER

1	2	3	4	5
6	**7**	**8**	**9**	**10**
11	**12**	**13**	**14**	**15**
16	**17**	**18**	**19**	**20**
21	**22**	**23**	**24**	**25**
26	**27**	**28**	**29**	**30**
31	**TOTAL**			

BUDGET

MOTIVATIONS

TEMPTATIONS

EXCEPTIONS

REWARDS

DAILY NO-SPEND TRACKER

1	2	3	4	5
6	7	8	9	10
11	12	13	14	15
16	17	18	19	20
21	22	23	24	25
26	27	28	29	30
31	TOTAL			

BUDGET

MOTIVATIONS

TEMPTATIONS

EXCEPTIONS

REWARDS

DAILY NO-SPEND TRACKER

1	2	3	4	5
6	7	8	9	10
11	12	13	14	15
16	17	18	19	20
21	22	23	24	25
26	27	28	29	30
31	TOTAL			

BUDGET

MOTIVATIONS

TEMPTATIONS

EXCEPTIONS

REWARDS

DAILY NO-SPEND TRACKER

1	2	3	4	5
6	7	8	9	10
11	12	13	14	15
16	17	18	19	20
21	22	23	24	25
26	27	28	29	30
31	TOTAL			

BUDGET

MOTIVATIONS

TEMPTATIONS

EXCEPTIONS

REWARDS

DAILY NO-SPEND TRACKER

1	2	3	4	5
6	7	8	9	10
11	12	13	14	15
16	17	18	19	20
21	22	23	24	25
26	27	28	29	30
31	TOTAL			

BUDGET

MOTIVATIONS

TEMPTATIONS

EXCEPTIONS

REWARDS

DAILY NO-SPEND TRACKER

1	2	3	4	5
6	7	8	9	10
11	12	13	14	15
16	17	18	19	20
21	22	23	24	25
26	27	28	29	30
31	TOTAL			

BUDGET

MOTIVATIONS

TEMPTATIONS

EXCEPTIONS

REWARDS

DAILY NO-SPEND TRACKER

1	2	3	4	5
6	7	8	9	10
11	12	13	14	15
16	17	18	19	20
21	22	23	24	25
26	27	28	29	30
31	TOTAL			

BUDGET

MOTIVATIONS

TEMPTATIONS

EXCEPTIONS

REWARDS

DAILY NO-SPEND TRACKER

1	2	3	4	5
6	7	8	9	10
11	12	13	14	15
16	17	18	19	20
21	22	23	24	25
26	27	28	29	30
31	TOTAL			

BUDGET

MOTIVATIONS

TEMPTATIONS

EXCEPTIONS

REWARDS

DAILY NO-SPEND TRACKER

1	2	3	4	5
6	**7**	**8**	**9**	**10**
11	**12**	**13**	**14**	**15**
16	**17**	**18**	**19**	**20**
21	**22**	**23**	**24**	**25**
26	**27**	**28**	**29**	**30**
31	**TOTAL**			

BUDGET

MOTIVATIONS

TEMPTATIONS

EXCEPTIONS

REWARDS

DAILY NO-SPEND TRACKER

1	2	3	4	5
6	**7**	**8**	**9**	**10**
11	**12**	**13**	**14**	**15**
16	**17**	**18**	**19**	**20**
21	**22**	**23**	**24**	**25**
26	**27**	**28**	**29**	**30**
31	**TOTAL**			

BUDGET

MOTIVATIONS

TEMPTATIONS

EXCEPTIONS

REWARDS

DAILY NO-SPEND TRACKER

1	2	3	4	5
6	7	8	9	10
11	12	13	14	15
16	17	18	19	20
21	22	23	24	25
26	27	28	29	30
31	TOTAL			

BUDGET

MOTIVATIONS

TEMPTATIONS

EXCEPTIONS

REWARDS

DAILY NO-SPEND TRACKER

1	2	3	4	5
6	7	8	9	10
11	12	13	14	15
16	17	18	19	20
21	22	23	24	25
26	27	28	29	30
31	TOTAL			

BUDGET

MOTIVATIONS

TEMPTATIONS

EXCEPTIONS

REWARDS

DAILY NO-SPEND TRACKER

1	2	3	4	5
6	7	8	9	10
11	12	13	14	15
16	17	18	19	20
21	22	23	24	25
26	27	28	29	30
31	TOTAL			

BUDGET

MOTIVATIONS

TEMPTATIONS

EXCEPTIONS

REWARDS

DAILY NO-SPEND TRACKER

1	2	3	4	5
6	7	8	9	10
11	12	13	14	15
16	17	18	19	20
21	22	23	24	25
26	27	28	29	30
31	TOTAL			

BUDGET

MOTIVATIONS

TEMPTATIONS

EXCEPTIONS

REWARDS

DAILY NO-SPEND TRACKER

1	2	3	4	5
6	7	8	9	10
11	12	13	14	15
16	17	18	19	20
21	22	23	24	25
26	27	28	29	30
31	TOTAL			

BUDGET

MOTIVATIONS

TEMPTATIONS

EXCEPTIONS

REWARDS

DAILY NO-SPEND TRACKER

1	2	3	4	5

6	7	8	9	10

11	12	13	14	15

16	17	18	19	20

21	22	23	24	25

26	27	28	29	30

31	TOTAL

BUDGET

MOTIVATIONS

TEMPTATIONS

EXCEPTIONS

REWARDS

DAILY NO-SPEND TRACKER

1	2	3	4	5
6	7	8	9	10
11	12	13	14	15
16	17	18	19	20
21	22	23	24	25
26	27	28	29	30
31	TOTAL			

BUDGET

MOTIVATIONS

TEMPTATIONS

EXCEPTIONS

REWARDS

DAILY NO-SPEND TRACKER

1	2	3	4	5
6	7	8	9	10
11	12	13	14	15
16	17	18	19	20
21	22	23	24	25
26	27	28	29	30
31	TOTAL			

BUDGET

MOTIVATIONS

TEMPTATIONS

EXCEPTIONS

REWARDS

DAILY NO-SPEND TRACKER

1	2	3	4	5
6	7	8	9	10
11	12	13	14	15
16	17	18	19	20
21	22	23	24	25
26	27	28	29	30
31	TOTAL			

BUDGET

MOTIVATIONS

TEMPTATIONS

EXCEPTIONS

REWARDS

DAILY NO-SPEND TRACKER

1	2	3	4	5

6	7	8	9	10

11	12	13	14	15

16	17	18	19	20

21	22	23	24	25

26	27	28	29	30

31	TOTAL

BUDGET

MOTIVATIONS

TEMPTATIONS

EXCEPTIONS

REWARDS

DAILY NO-SPEND TRACKER

1	2	3	4	5
6	7	8	9	10
11	12	13	14	15
16	17	18	19	20
21	22	23	24	25
26	27	28	29	30
31	TOTAL			

BUDGET

MOTIVATIONS

TEMPTATIONS

EXCEPTIONS

REWARDS

DAILY NO-SPEND TRACKER

1	2	3	4	5
6	**7**	**8**	**9**	**10**
11	**12**	**13**	**14**	**15**
16	**17**	**18**	**19**	**20**
21	**22**	**23**	**24**	**25**
26	**27**	**28**	**29**	**30**
31	**TOTAL**			

BUDGET

MOTIVATIONS

TEMPTATIONS

EXCEPTIONS

REWARDS

DAILY NO-SPEND TRACKER

1	2	3	4	5

6	7	8	9	10

11	12	13	14	15

16	17	18	19	20

21	22	23	24	25

26	27	28	29	30

31	TOTAL

BUDGET

MOTIVATIONS

TEMPTATIONS

EXCEPTIONS

REWARDS

DAILY NO-SPEND TRACKER

1	2	3	4	5
6	**7**	**8**	**9**	**10**
11	**12**	**13**	**14**	**15**
16	**17**	**18**	**19**	**20**
21	**22**	**23**	**24**	**25**
26	**27**	**28**	**29**	**30**
31	**TOTAL**			

BUDGET

MOTIVATIONS

TEMPTATIONS

EXCEPTIONS

REWARDS

DAILY NO-SPEND TRACKER

1	2	3	4	5
6	7	8	9	10
11	12	13	14	15
16	17	18	19	20
21	22	23	24	25
26	27	28	29	30
31	TOTAL			

BUDGET

MOTIVATIONS

TEMPTATIONS

EXCEPTIONS

REWARDS

DAILY NO-SPEND TRACKER

1	2	3	4	5
6	7	8	9	10
11	12	13	14	15
16	17	18	19	20
21	22	23	24	25
26	27	28	29	30
31	TOTAL			

BUDGET

MOTIVATIONS

TEMPTATIONS

EXCEPTIONS

REWARDS

DAILY NO-SPEND TRACKER

1	2	3	4	5
6	7	8	9	10
11	12	13	14	15
16	17	18	19	20
21	22	23	24	25
26	27	28	29	30
31	TOTAL			

BUDGET

MOTIVATIONS

TEMPTATIONS

EXCEPTIONS

REWARDS

DAILY NO-SPEND TRACKER

1	2	3	4	5

6	7	8	9	10

11	12	13	14	15

16	17	18	19	20

21	22	23	24	25

26	27	28	29	30

31	TOTAL

BUDGET

MOTIVATIONS

TEMPTATIONS

EXCEPTIONS

REWARDS

DAILY NO-SPEND TRACKER

1	2	3	4	5
6	7	8	9	10
11	12	13	14	15
16	17	18	19	20
21	22	23	24	25
26	27	28	29	30
31	TOTAL			

BUDGET

MOTIVATIONS

TEMPTATIONS

EXCEPTIONS

REWARDS

DAILY NO-SPEND TRACKER

1	2	3	4	5
6	**7**	**8**	**9**	**10**
11	**12**	**13**	**14**	**15**
16	**17**	**18**	**19**	**20**
21	**22**	**23**	**24**	**25**
26	**27**	**28**	**29**	**30**
31	**TOTAL**			

BUDGET

MOTIVATIONS

TEMPTATIONS

EXCEPTIONS

REWARDS

DAILY NO-SPEND TRACKER

1	2	3	4	5
6	**7**	**8**	**9**	**10**
11	**12**	**13**	**14**	**15**
16	**17**	**18**	**19**	**20**
21	**22**	**23**	**24**	**25**
26	**27**	**28**	**29**	**30**
31	**TOTAL**			

BUDGET

MOTIVATIONS

TEMPTATIONS

EXCEPTIONS

REWARDS

DAILY NO-SPEND TRACKER

1	2	3	4	5
6	**7**	**8**	**9**	**10**
11	**12**	**13**	**14**	**15**
16	**17**	**18**	**19**	**20**
21	**22**	**23**	**24**	**25**
26	**27**	**28**	**29**	**30**
31	**TOTAL**			

BUDGET

MOTIVATIONS

TEMPTATIONS

EXCEPTIONS

REWARDS

DAILY NO-SPEND TRACKER

1	2	3	4	5
6	**7**	**8**	**9**	**10**
11	**12**	**13**	**14**	**15**
16	**17**	**18**	**19**	**20**
21	**22**	**23**	**24**	**25**
26	**27**	**28**	**29**	**30**
31	**TOTAL**			

BUDGET

MOTIVATIONS

TEMPTATIONS

EXCEPTIONS

REWARDS

DAILY NO-SPEND TRACKER

1	2	3	4	5

6	7	8	9	10

11	12	13	14	15

16	17	18	19	20

21	22	23	24	25

26	27	28	29	30

31	TOTAL

BUDGET

MOTIVATIONS

TEMPTATIONS

EXCEPTIONS

REWARDS

DAILY NO-SPEND TRACKER

1	2	3	4	5

6	7	8	9	10

11	12	13	14	15

16	17	18	19	20

21	22	23	24	25

26	27	28	29	30

31	TOTAL

BUDGET

MOTIVATIONS

TEMPTATIONS

EXCEPTIONS

REWARDS

10 TIPS FOR SAVING MONEY

1. Shop at discount food stores: To save money on groceries, find discount grocery stores in your neighborhood. In these shops, you can frequently find things at lower prices.

2. Purchase in bulk: Non-perishable goods can help you save money over time if you buy them in large quantities. Consider buying at a wholesale club or look for bulk selections at your local grocery store.

3. Take advantage of loyalty programs: Several retailers have programs that reward customers with discounts, coupons, or other benefits. Join these programs to receive discounts on your purchases.

4. Rent instead of buy: Take into account renting tools or clothing for special occasions if you only require them for a short time. By doing this, you can avoid paying full price for these things.

5. Repair rather than replace: If something breaks, think about having it repaired rather than purchasing a new one. This can help you save money and cut down on trash.

6. Buy used goods: Browse online markets or thrift shops for used goods like furniture or apparel. These goods are frequently far less expensive than brand-new ones.

7. Reduce subscriptions: Take an inventory of your monthly subscriptions and cancel any you don't use or need. You can do this to save money each month.

8. Purchase generic or store-brand goods: Rather than spending money on name-brand goods, consider purchasing generic or store-brand goods. Often, they are just as good but less expensive.

9. Disconnect from the TV: Viewing less TV can help you spend less on streaming or cable services. Instead, look for cost-free activities to keep you entertained, like reading a book or taking a walk.

10. Take part in a cashback program. Certain credit cards or apps give back money when you make a purchase. Find these programs and take advantage of them to get cash back on your weekly shopping.

Weekly
SAVINGS

WEEKLY SAVINGS

	AMOUNT SAVED	BALANCE
1		
2		
3		
4		
5		
6		
7		
8		
9		
10		
11		
12		
13		
14		
15		
16		
17		
18		
19		
20		
21		
22		
23		
24		
25		
26		

TOTAL:

WEEKLY SAVINGS

	AMOUNT SAVED	BALANCE
27		
28		
29		
30		
31		
32		
33		
34		
35		
36		
37		
38		
39		
40		
41		
42		
43		
44		
45		
46		
47		
48		
49		
50		
51		
52		

TOTAL:

WEEKLY SAVINGS

	AMOUNT SAVED	BALANCE
1		
2		
3		
4		
5		
6		
7		
8		
9		
10		
11		
12		
13		
14		
15		
16		
17		
18		
19		
20		
21		
22		
23		
24		
25		
26		

TOTAL:

WEEKLY SAVINGS

	AMOUNT SAVED	BALANCE
27		
28		
29		
30		
31		
32		
33		
34		
35		
36		
37		
38		
39		
40		
41		
42		
43		
44		
45		
46		
47		
48		
49		
50		
51		
52		

TOTAL:

WEEKLY SAVINGS

	AMOUNT SAVED	BALANCE
1		
2		
3		
4		
5		
6		
7		
8		
9		
10		
11		
12		
13		
14		
15		
16		
17		
18		
19		
20		
21		
22		
23		
24		
25		
26		

TOTAL:

WEEKLY SAVINGS

	AMOUNT SAVED	BALANCE
27		
28		
29		
30		
31		
32		
33		
34		
35		
36		
37		
38		
39		
40		
41		
42		
43		
44		
45		
46		
47		
48		
49		
50		
51		
52		

TOTAL:

WEEKLY SAVINGS

	AMOUNT SAVED	BALANCE
1		
2		
3		
4		
5		
6		
7		
8		
9		
10		
11		
12		
13		
14		
15		
16		
17		
18		
19		
20		
21		
22		
23		
24		
25		
26		

TOTAL:

WEEKLY SAVINGS

	AMOUNT SAVED	BALANCE
27		
28		
29		
30		
31		
32		
33		
34		
35		
36		
37		
38		
39		
40		
41		
42		
43		
44		
45		
46		
47		
48		
49		
50		
51		
52		

TOTAL:

10 MORE TIPS FOR SAVING MONEY

1. Switch to a lower-cost cell phone plan: Shop around for a more affordable cell phone plan that fits your needs. Consider switching to a prepaid plan or a family plan to save money.

2. Reduce utility bills: Save money on your utility bills by turning off lights and electronics when you're not using them, taking shorter showers, and lowering the temperature on your hot water heater.

3. Use a refillable water bottle: Stop buying bottled water and instead use a refillable water bottle. This can save you money and reduce waste.

4. Make your own cleaning products: Instead of buying expensive cleaning products, try making your own using simple ingredients such as vinegar and baking soda.

5. Make your own personal care products: Instead of buying expensive personal care products, try making your own using natural ingredients such as coconut oil or honey.

6. Shop for insurance: Shop around for car and home insurance to make sure you're getting the best rate. Consider bundling policies to save even more.

7. Negotiate bills: Call your service providers and negotiate your bills. You may be able to get a lower rate or a promotional offer.

8. Use a cashback credit card: Use a credit card that offers cashback on purchases to earn money back on your monthly spending. Just make sure to pay off your balance in full each month to avoid interest charges.

9. Use a cash envelope system: Use a cash envelope system to help you stick to your budget. Divide your monthly spending into categories and put cash in separate envelopes for each category. This can help you avoid overspending.

10. Avoid impulse purchases: Try to avoid impulse purchases by waiting at least 24 hours before making a purchase. This can help you avoid buying items you don't really need or want.

Monthly
SAVINGS

MONTHLY SAVINGS

JAN	FEB	MAR
APR	MAY	JUN
JUL	AUG	SEPT
OCT	NOV	DEC

GOAL

JAN	FEB	MAR
APR	**MAY**	**JUN**
JUL	**AUG**	**SEPT**
OCT	**NOV**	**DEC**

TOTAL YEAR SAVINGS:

SAVINGS JAR GAME

$100 | $5 | BUY YOUR FAVORITE BEVERAGE YOU'RE ON THE RIGHT PATH! | $20 | $10 | MOVE FORWARD 3 SPACES +SAVE $10 EXTRA | $25

$20 | $50 | $5 | $25 | GIVE YOURSELF THE GIFT OF LEARNING SOMETHING NEW!

GOAL:

100%
90%
80%
70%
60%
50%
40%
30%
20%
10%

$20 | $10 | TREAT YOURSELF WITH YOUR FAVORITE DESSERT! | $50 | $25

$50 | $20 | $100 | $5 | MOVE FORWARD 9 SPACES +SAVE $10 EXTRA | $10 | GO! $5

ROLE THE DICE, MOVE SPACES, ADD THE AMOUNT TO YOUR SAVINGS JAR!
DO THIS EVERY WEEK FOR A YEAR AND SAVE AT LEAST $1000!

WEEKLY SAVINGS

2	3	4	5	6	7	8	9	10
12	13	14	15	16	17	18	19	20
22	23	24	25	26	27	28	29	30
32	33	34	35	36	37	38	39	40
42	43	44	45	46	47	48	49	50

MONTHLY SAVINGS

JAN	FEB	MAR
APR	MAY	JUN
JUL	AUG	SEPT
OCT	NOV	DEC

GOAL

JAN	FEB	MAR
APR	MAY	JUN
JUL	AUG	SEPT
OCT	NOV	DEC

TOTAL YEAR SAVINGS:

SAVINGS JAR GAME

GO! $5

$10

MOVE FORWARD 9 SPACES +SAVE $10 EXTRA

$5

$100

$20

$50

GIVE YOURSELF THE GIFT OF LEARNING SOMETHING NEW!

$25

$5

$50

$20

$100

$5

BUY YOUR FAVORITE BEVERAGE YOU'RE ON THE RIGHT PATH!

$20

$10

MOVE FORWARD 3 SPACES +SAVE $10 EXTRA

$25

$20

$10

TREAT YOURSELF WITH YOUR FAVORITE DESSERT!

$50

$25

GOAL:

100%

90%

80%

70%

60%

50%

40%

30%

20%

10%

ROLE THE DICE, MOVE SPACES, ADD THE AMOUNT TO YOUR SAVINGS JAR!
DO THIS EVERY WEEK FOR A YEAR AND SAVE AT LEAST $1000!

WEEKLY SAVINGS

1	2	3	4	5	6	7	8	9	10
11	12	13	14	15	16	17	18	19	20
21	22	23	24	25	26	27	28	29	30
31	32	33	34	35	36	37	38	39	40
41	42	43	44	45	46	47	48	49	50

MONTHLY SAVINGS

GOAL

JAN	FEB	MAR
APR	**MAY**	**JUN**
JUL	**AUG**	**SEPT**
OCT	**NOV**	**DEC**

TOTAL YEAR SAVINGS:

SAVINGS JAR GAME

$100

$5

BUY YOUR FAVORITE BEVERAGE YOU'RE ON THE RIGHT PATH!

$20

$10

MOVE FORWARD 3 SPACES +SAVE $10 EXTRA

$25

$20

$50

$5

$25

GIVE YOURSELF THE GIFT OF LEARNING SOMETHING NEW!

GOAL:

100%
90%
80%
70%
60%
50%
40%
30%
20%
10%

$20

$10

TREAT YOURSELF WITH YOUR FAVORITE DESSERT!

$50

$25

$50

$20

$100

$5

MOVE FORWARD 9 SPACES +SAVE $10 EXTRA

$10

GO! $5

ROLE THE DICE, MOVE SPACES, ADD THE AMOUNT TO YOUR SAVINGS JAR!
DO THIS EVERY WEEK FOR A YEAR AND SAVE AT LEAST $1000!

WEEKLY SAVINGS

1	2	3	4	5	6	7	8	9	10
11	12	13	14	15	16	17	18	19	20
21	22	23	24	25	26	27	28	29	30
31	32	33	34	35	36	37	38	39	40
41	42	43	44	45	46	47	48	49	50

MONTHLY SAVINGS

GOAL

JAN	FEB	MAR
APR	MAY	JUN
JUL	AUG	SEPT
OCT	NOV	DEC

TOTAL YEAR SAVINGS:

SAVINGS JAR GAME

$100	$5	BUY YOUR FAVORITE BEVERAGE YOU'RE ON THE RIGHT PATH!	$20	$10	MOVE FORWARD 3 SPACES +SAVE $10 EXTRA	$25
$20						$20
$50						$10
$5						TREAT YOURSELF WITH YOUR FAVORITE DESSERT!
$25						$50
GIVE YOURSELF THE GIFT OF LEARNING SOMETHING NEW!						$25
$50	$20	$100	$5	MOVE FORWARD 9 SPACES +SAVE $10 EXTRA	$10	GO! $5

GOAL:

______ 100%
______ 90%
______ 80%
______ 70%
______ 60%
______ 50%
______ 40%
______ 30%
______ 20%
______ 10%

ROLE THE DICE, MOVE SPACES, ADD THE AMOUNT TO YOUR SAVINGS JAR!
DO THIS EVERY WEEK FOR A YEAR AND SAVE AT LEAST $1000!

WEEKLY SAVINGS

2	3	4	5	6	7	8	9	10
12	13	14	15	16	17	18	19	20
22	23	24	25	26	27	28	29	30
32	33	34	35	36	37	38	39	40
42	43	44	45	46	47	48	49	50

Made in the USA
Monee, IL
04 November 2026

67377493R00056